A
Novice Trekker
in
Nepal

Ian Douglas

Dedication

Dedicated to

Andy Douglas

1982-2011

Andy passed on his love of Nepal to me.

Copyright

Text copyright © Ian Douglas 2014
Photographs copyright © Ian and Tim Douglas 2013
All rights reserved.

Acknowledgements

I would like to thank my wife Caroline Douglas, and Bryce Mansfield, for reviewing a draft of the text and for their useful comments.

ISBN-13: 978-1495318047

ISBN-10: 1495318044

A Novice Trekker in Nepal

Contents

1. INTRODUCTION 1
   - An Outline of Our Trip 2
2. THE TREK 7
   - Tea Houses and Porters 7
   - The First 6 Days Walking 9
   - About the Mountains 15
   - Back to the Trek 16
3. EXCURSIONS AND SIGHTSEEING 25
   - Pokhara 25
     - Phewa Tal Lake 26
     - International Mountain Museum 26
     - Devi's Falls and Gupteshwor Mahadev 28
     - Tibetan Refugee Camp 28
   - Chitwan 28
   - Kathmandu 32
     - Durbar Squares in Kathmandu and Patan 33
     - The Pashupatinath Hindu Temple Area 34
     - Buddhist Areas – Swayambhunath and Boudhanath 35
4. PRACTICAL ISSUES FOR THE TREKKER AND TOURIST 38
   - What Do You Need For Trekking In Nepal? 38
   - Personal Hygiene on Trek 41

Clothes Washing Facilities on Trek **41**

Water on Trek **42**

Money Changing **42**

Electricity and Wi-Fi **42**

Bargaining in Nepal **42**

Taxis **43**

Tipping **43**

5. WHAT EFFECT DID NEPAL HAVE ON ME? **44**

A NOVICE TREKKER IN NEPAL

1. INTRODUCTION

This book is not intended to replace much more detailed guides such as the Lonely Planet Guide or Rough Guide to Nepal. However for the first time trekker or visitor it can be difficult to see the wood from the trees when reading these books. The Lonely Planet and the Rough Guides are written by people with considerable knowledge of the country, but sometimes they can get overly complex and involved, covering a wide range of interests.

Instead this short book is intended to give advice to the novice trekker and visitor who could benefit from a more basic view before immersing in detail in the Lonely Planet or Rough Guide series. The book describes my trek to the Annapurna Sanctuary, and sightseeing in Kathmandu, Pokhara and Chitwan. I hope you will find some of the information in this book useful if you are planning to visit Nepal, or are just interested in this fascinating country.

This was my first visit to Nepal, and in three weeks I fell in love with the country and the Nepalese people. As in any country, tourists have to be on their guard up to a point, but I found the great majority of Nepalese charming. And although many people are very poor, most seem much more positive and happy with their lot than westerners. Their greeting of "Namaste", which you hear many times a day, is sometimes translated as "I salute the God within you", much preferable to our simple hello. A polite thank you from a westerner invariably gets the response of "welcome" from a Nepalese, even a young child.

Nepal is a country of 27 million people. It is a landlocked country, with India on its western, southern and eastern borders. China's Tibetan Autonomous Region (formerly Tibet) is on its northern border. It is therefore sandwiched between two global powers, whose relationship hasn't always been easy. Nepal is about 800 kilometres (500 miles) long and 200 kilometres (125 miles) wide.

The low lying plains in the south, the Terai, have areas of sub-tropical jungle. Nepal's National Parks, such as the world famous Chitwan, have a variety of fascinating and often endangered wildlife. Moving north, the land gets higher. The north of the country is part of the Great Himalayan mountain range. Although a small country Nepal has eight of the fourteen 8,000 metre plus (26,247 ft.) peaks in the world. In fact, Nepal is trying to get a further 5 peaks recognised as over 8000 metres – these are sub-peaks of other recognised 8000m peaks.

Unlike most of Europe it did not suffer grievous damage from bombing in the Second World War and therefore many key historic sights continue to exist in the two cities we visited. However much of Nepal did suffer from a devastating earthquake in 1934.

Spellings of place names in Nepal can differ in books and maps, because translating the local name from Devanagari script to Roman script has not always been done consistently. I have tried to use what I understand to be the common spelling, but some texts may use slightly different spelling.

An Outline of Our Trip

My visit was in October and November 2013. October and November are considered good months to trek, after the summer monsoon but before the intense cold of winter. March and April are also good months, when the rhododendrons are blooming in the Annapurna foothills. We flew to Nepal's capital Kathmandu, spent a day sightseeing, and then flew to Pokhara to embark on the Annapurna Sanctuary trek.

There are several classic Annapurna treks. The Annapurna Circuit is a trek around the outside of the Annapurna mountain range. A further classic trek takes you into the Annapurna foothills, probably making the viewpoint on Poon Hill (3210 metres), the summit of the trek. The third classic, the Annapurna Sanctuary trek, is the one we undertook. It goes through the foothills, and then goes on further up the deep and narrow Modi Valley from Chhromrong, to the Annapurna Sanctuary.

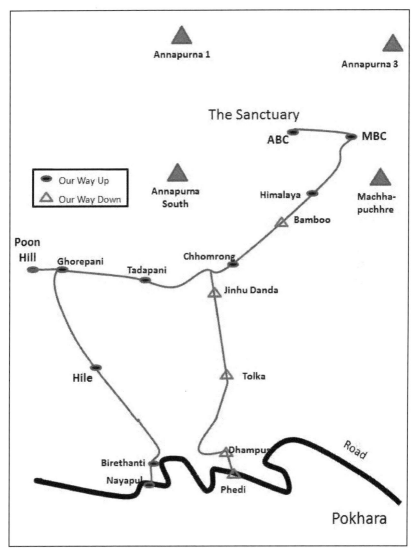

Pic 1. A schematic map of our trek to the Annapurna Sanctuary

The Sanctuary is a high, relatively flat area at 4100 metres surrounded by mountains. Since the valley created by the Modi exiting from the Sanctuary is narrow and deep, it is difficult to see from the middle of the Sanctuary. Therefore the Sanctuary appears to be totally surrounded by 7,000 and 8,000 metre mountains. It is often referred to as a natural amphitheatre, and the area has religious significance to Hindus.

The trek is also known as the Annapurna Base Camp trek, because the small group of teahouses in the middle of the Sanctuary is known as Annapurna Base Camp (often abbreviated to ABC). ABC is the site of the camp where climbing expeditions based themselves when attempting some of the mountains in the Annapurna range.

I flew from the UK, via Dubai and Delhi on Emirates, an excellent airline. Then from Delhi to Kathmandu on Air India, o.k. but not the same quality. I arrived at Kathmandu airport at about 9a.m., after over 24 hours travelling. I had to spend an hour in the immigration queue, which is particularly annoying when you are tired after a long flight. In future I recommend downloading the visa application form from the Nepalese government website and bringing the form completed. This allows you to get an early place in the queue for a visa whilst other passengers are completing forms they have collected in the airport. I was met at the airport by my son Tim who had travelled to Kathmandu a few days earlier, and by Govinda Sapkota, our guide. Govinda had been recommended to us, and we had arranged the trek via e-mail. His website is www.nepaltrekplanner.com and has some excellent photos of Nepal.

We went to the hotel and after a break to recover from the flight did some sightseeing in Kathmandu in the afternoon. The main sites we visited in Kathmandu are described in Chapter 3.

After the trek we did some sightseeing in Pokhara, and then drove to the Chitwan National Park, spending two nights there. Then on to Kathmandu where we spent another two days sightseeing, before returning home.

Our party consisted of three trekkers, our guide and two porters. I am a man in my sixties, and have had numerous operations and procedures since 2010 for neuroendocrine cancer, the cancer that Steve Jobs of Apple had. I do not see myself as particularly fit. I am not usually a walker although I did a number of walks in preparation for the trek. Normally my only commitment to fitness is that I cycle 60 miles or so a week. The trek isn't easy, but providing you train appropriately beforehand most people should be able to manage it.

Based on the number of flagstone steps we had to walk up on the trek, people living or working in the upper floors of multi-storey buildings are in an excellent position to prepare, by walking up the stairs rather than taking the lift!

Pic 2. Some of the steps.

My travelling companions were my son Tim, our excellent Nepalese guide Govinda, and Genevieve, a Belgian young lady who we didn't know before the trek but who approached Govinda at the same time as we did.

For the trek, Govinda hired two porters, Tharpule and Mahesha, and they joined us in Pokhara. Govinda had used Tharpule and Mahesha before, and they did an excellent job for us.

Chapter 2 of this book describes our trek to the Annapurna Sanctuary.

Chapter 3 describes our sightseeing excursions in Kathmandu, Chitwan and Pokhara.

Chapter 4 outlines some practical issues for the trekker and tourist in Nepal, including what I think the trekker needs to take.

Chapter 5 finishes with my observations on holidaying in Nepal.

2. THE TREK

Tea Houses and Porters

Tea houses are your accommodation, resting and eating places on trek. On the Annapurna Sanctuary trek tea houses are generally no more than two hours apart. Therefore you are unlikely to be more than an hour from a tea house. Useful to know if things get rough.

Tea houses are usually very basic accommodation. They can also be referred to as guest houses, although some are as basic as hostels. I will call them tea houses. No tea house we stayed in had any heating in the bedrooms. Rooms generally only have beds, often very close together to make the best use of space. A few have electric lighting in the rooms; many don't. The only heating available was often a wood stove in the communal dining room. Water could be heated by the wood stove, but the stove would generally only be set alight from the early evening.

Pic 3. Typical tea house bedroom for three.

Whilst some only had wood stoves, others had gas or solar heating for hot water. If solar heating was used, the water which was heated during the day would be quickly used up by the first few trekkers arriving in the afternoon. Therefore get into the showers as quickly as possible when you arrive. I also suggest that irrespective of the form of heating you confirm that hot water is coming from the shower before getting undressed. If there is no hot water, you might want to reconsider! Invariably the shower cubicles opened directly into the open, so even if you have a hot shower it could be very cold when drying.

Many tea houses stated on boards outside that they had Wi-Fi. This was notional Wi-Fi. It frequently didn't work.

On a more positive note the food available was basic but okay and inexpensive by western standards.

Pic 4. Porters walking to the Sanctuary. I thought I had some hard jobs in the past, but I am not so sure now! Some porters wore trainers.

The higher you get on the trek, the more basic the tea houses become. It is not a question of paying more for a better standard of accommodation – there just aren't any.

Porters, guides, and staff often slept in the communal dining room. At the Annapurna Base Camp, in the tea house where we stayed, 41 people had to sleep in the rather small communal dining room. That included six trekkers who could not be accommodated in bedrooms. We were lucky; there were only three of us in our tiny room.

Each of us gave our porters 10 kilos or more to carry, and the porters had to carry their own much scanter packs. Govinda carried his own pack. Therefore the porters were carrying 20 kilos or more each. I understand the accepted maximum is 25 kilos. Please see chapter 4 – Practical Issues for the Trekker and Tourist for what I believe the trekker needs.

The First 6 Days Walking

We got up early in Kathmandu on Thursday, 24 October to travel to the airport for a flight to Pokhara, a major Nepalese city within sight of the Annapurna range. The plane was small, taking only 18 passengers. We had almost to crawl along the aisle to get to our seats. With the benefit of experience it would have been better to sit on the right side of the aircraft - the view of the mountains would have been better when landing in Pokhara.

We spent the rest of the day sightseeing in Pokhara, and I describe this later in chapter 3. At Pokhara we stayed in the Rustika Hotel, in an en-suite room. We weren't going to have an en-suite room again until Dhampus on the way back. We were able to leave any belongings we wouldn't need on the trek in the Rustika, and collect them on the way back, and I had brought a lockable bag for this purpose.

The following morning we drove to Nayapul, about an hour and a half from Pokhara. Nayapul is a common trail dropping off point for the Annapurna Sanctuary trek. Some people start the trek from Phedi and end it at Nayapul, but we started at Nayapul and ended at Phedi, which gave us about a day extra to acclimatise before breaching 4000 metres.

Nayapul has all of the usual small market stalls selling tat and knock off hiking gear. We then walked to Birethanti (1050 metres altitude), where there is a TIMS (Trekkers' Information Management System) check point. At the checkpoint you have to pay a fee (currently the Nepal currency equivalent of $10 a person if with a guide and $20 if an individual trekker), and register some details of the trek. The difference in fee is a minor encouragement to book a guide.

Shortly after Birethanti the road stops and there are only walking trails. From then on everything required, whether by trekkers or the local population, has to be carried by donkeys or by porters. We saw a number of donkey trains over the next days, and porters carrying trekkers' luggage. If the porters were not carrying rucksacks they had dokos (very large wicker baskets) on their backs full of supplies for the local people or the tea houses. The rest of the day was a long and tiring walk to our first overnight stop at a tea house in Hile, where we spent the night.

The trails on the Annapurna Sanctuary trek were generally good and well kept, with many flights of steps flagged. That is one of the things you will remember from the trek – the seemingly endless flights of flagstone steps. It can be quite a walk uphill.

Day 2, Saturday 26th October. A long hard walk to Hill Top tea house in Ghorepani. We had no problem sleeping after that day's walk, and we planned to get up early the next day.

Day 3, Sunday 27th. We were up at 4.45a.m. – it was easy to wake up though, as the tea house was a hive of activity. We joined a line of trekkers with head torches making their way up Poon Hill, a classic viewpoint on the trek. This involved a two kilometre walk, largely uphill, from the tea house, and paying a small charge at one point. We were like a line of ants, making our way uphill in the dark, only able to see the distance of the next head torch forward. It was an exhausting walk up stone steps to the relatively flat hill top at 3210 metres. There was a viewing area at the top, and a viewing platform. I estimate 400 people had made the journey that morning to see the dawn from Poon Hill.

The views as dawn broke were stunning. The sun glinted orange and crimson on the snow-covered Annapurna range – a sight I will remember forever.

Pic 5. A View from Poon Hill at Dawn

The walk down was much easier than the way up! We spent the rest of the day in Ghorepani, whilst many hardier walkers continued on their trek.

The trekkers we met were a great mixture of nationalities and ages. There were more Asian trekkers than westerners, mainly Chinese, Japanese, Taiwanese, Indians, and South Koreans. Westerners included French, British, Danish, Czech, Canadian, American and Australian. Some people were travelling alone, but most were in guide-led groups.

Day 4, Monday 28th, another hard walk. We started immediately uphill at quite a pace. I had diarrhoea, possibly because I was gasping in large quantities of air as I exerted myself to keep up with our little group of younger and fitter walkers. I was totally exhausted by the end of the day. We stayed in a fairly basic tea house in Tadapani. However there was an excellent sunset and sunrise.

There are many rhododendron forests in the area. Not rhododendron bushes as you get in the UK, but forests of trees which looked to be 20 metres (65 feet) high. The rhododendron is the national flower of

Nepal. Unfortunately they bloom from March to May, so in October/November we did not see them at their best. Apparently Nepal has 30 species of rhododendron.

*Pic 6. There are many bridges like this.
And they sway as you walk across them!*

Day 5, Tuesday 29th. We descended from Tadapani across some fairly scary bridges. You encounter two types of bridge on the Annapurna Sanctuary trek. The traditional rope suspension bridge has been replaced by steel wire suspension bridges. These are no doubt safer, but they still rock from side to side as you walk across. I am afraid of heights, and shared my concerns with Govinda our guide. Govinda offered to help by doing what the Nepalese do to get livestock across narrow or dangerous bridges; that is blindfolding me and leading me across. I turned down his kind offer and gathered together what little courage I had.

The second type of bridge is used on narrow streams where the path goes down to the stream. It consists of two logs across the stream, with planks attached between them, and rocks on the planks to give it stability. They are frightening too if the stream is fast flowing and only a few inches below the bridge.

Pic 7. The low bridges can be frightening too, particularly if the stream, often just a few inches below the bridge, is fast flowing

Then up more steps to an upmarket (for tea houses) lodge in Chhomrong (2210m). The bedrooms were slightly bigger and better. The area around Chhomrong is heavily farmed, with spectacular terracing on the steep slopes. We were now down at 2170 metres, a drop of over 1000 metres from the top of Poon Hill. Because various routes in the foothills to Chhomrong are now channelled into one route up the narrow Modi valley, the route now got busier and the lodges fuller. For the first time Genevieve had to share a room with Tim and me because the tea house was full.

I should point out that Genevieve is a vegetarian. However, this did not stop her asking us to despatch the occasional creepy crawly that that she found in her part of the room.

Day 6, Wednesday the 30th October, (although what day of the week it was no longer mattered). We left the heavily populated area and continued walking up the Modi valley, which had narrowed considerably, towards the Annapurna Base Camp and Sanctuary. Leaving Chhomrong the trail has a major descent, followed by a climb, and then another descent and climb. Now we were in an area that wasn't farmed, and which has religious significance for Hindus. In fact we soon came across the following sign:

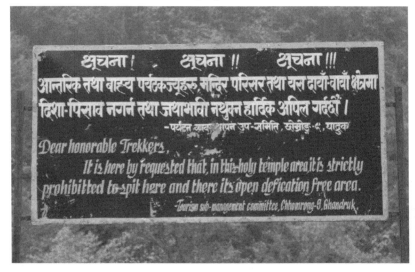

Pic 8. *We were entering an area with religious significance for Hindus.*

We had lunch in the small complex of teashops called Bamboo (2310 metres). In spite of all our exertions up and down, we had only ascended a net height of 100 metres in the morning! This is where Govinda introduced me to the concept of Nepali flat – the net ascent is negligible although the total ascent and descent is considerable!

In the afternoon we walked to a fairly basic lodge in the grouping of tea houses called Himalaya. Half an hour before we arrived a torrential storm started. The porters got out PVC ponchos, which they used to cover their bodies and the packs on their backs. The storm lasted all night, but when we woke in the morning it was sunny and cold. We were lucky; this was the only substantial rainstorm during our trek, but on two occasions we had brief hailstorms, with very large lumps of hail.

About the Mountains

Now that we were in the gorge of the River Modi, I would like to say a little about the area and the mountains, one of the prime reasons for us being here.

The upper Modi valley and the Annapurna Sanctuary were unknown to westerners until 1956, when James Roberts, a British army officer and climber, travelled up the gorge to the Sanctuary when reconnoitring for the 1957 Machhapuchhare expedition. Prior to Roberts' reconnoitre of the area the Sanctuary was only known to a few herdsmen who periodically grazed their flocks there.

The main mountains in the Annapurna range are:

Annapurna 1	8091m (26,545ft). The 10th highest mountain in the world.
Annapurna 2	7,937m (26,040ft)
Annapurna 3	7,555m (24,786ft)
Annapurna 4	7,525m (24,688ft)
Annapurna South	7,219m (24,688ft)
Machhapuchhare	6,993m (22,943ft)

To put these heights in perspective:

Mount Everest is 8,848m (29,029ft).

Ben Nevis, the U.K's highest mountain is *1,344M* (4,409ft).

Mount Whitney, the highest mountain in the contiguous United States is 4,421m (14,505ft).

Mount McKinley, the highest mountain in Alaska, is 6,194m (20,320ft).

Several hours' walk before Annapurna Base Camp, is Machhapuchhare Base Camp (or MBC as it is often abbreviated to). Machhapuchhare is a spectacular peak, seeming to rise almost vertically into the sky in places. It has a double summit, and hence looks like a fish tail, which is what Machhapuchhare means in Nepali. It is often referred to as fish tail, as this is much easier for visitors to pronounce.

Machhapuchhare has never been fully climbed. In 1957 British climbers Wilfred Noyce and David Cox deliberately stopped 50 metres short of the summit, because of the religious significance of the mountain.

Machhapuchhare has now been declared sacred and Nepal will not allow climbing on it. See http://www.himalayanclub.org/journal/machhapuchhare/ for the background and a description of Noyce and Cox's climb.

Annapurna 1 was the first 8,000m plus mountain in the world to be climbed to the summit, although British climbers had ascended to 8500m from the 1920s in attempts on Everest. Everest wasn't summited until 1953. In 1950 French climbers Maurice Herzog and Louis Lachenal climbed Annapurna 1. Both lost their toes, and Herzog lost many of his fingers to frostbite. Herzog dictated "Annapurna", still the best selling ever mountaineering book, about the expedition.

Since then, Annapurna 1 has claimed a higher fatality rate of climbers than any other 8000m peak. As of March 2012 there had been 191 successful ascents and 61 deaths, a fatality rate of 32% of the successful climbs. It may have a higher fatality rate than Everest, for example, because Everest is far busier and therefore has long-established routes and a very experienced set of guides.

Back to the Trek

Day 7, Thursday 31st. We walked from our overnight stop in a tea house in Himalaya and stopped in Deuval for lemon tea, and then on to Machhapuchhare Base Camp (MBC). At least on this leg we didn't have the frustration of going down and up. It was largely all up from 2920 metres at Himalaya to 3700 metres at Machhapuchhare.

Pic 9. The Upper Modi Valley

We went into the dining room at MBC to find a British scientist sitting at the communal dining table dissecting a shrew. To be fair, he did offer to stop, but being polite Brits we said we were happy for him to continue. He seemed to make a habit of capturing and killing small animals, having a whole host of traps for small mammals.

This was a great opportunity to ask a scientist who knew the Himalayas about the Yeti. His view was that it was not possible that a large mammal could have survived unnoticed in the Himalayas, because of the number of people climbing and trekking in the mountains in the last few decades. He briefly discussed this with to a Nepalese scientist colleague who was part of their group. They both agreed. Shrews were much more interesting than Yeti in the British scientist's opinion. Ah, the lack of romance in the scientific community. No wonder young people today are giving science a miss. I spent some of the rest of the day reflecting on this, including when I was having my evening meal at the table upon which he had dissected the shrew.

The Machhapuchhare tea house was the first opportunity for several days for a shower - it had a gas heated shower system. It is interesting having a shower in a small unheated shower room with gaps in the walls near the rafters, and a door that opens directly into the open air, where the temperature is zero degrees centigrade. You do dry yourself rather quickly.

Anyone ascending to the sort of height we had should be aware of the risk of acute mountain sickness, also known as altitude sickness. In extreme cases it can be fatal. However, our ascent was relatively slow, if only because I wasn't fit enough to do it much faster! So although our breathing was now increasingly laboured, we didn't encounter any problems at this altitude, and nor did anyone we met.

Pic 10. Annapurna Base Camp on 1st November before a night of snow.

Day 8, Friday 1st November, was **the day**. The walk to Annapurna Base Camp (or ABC to the cognoscenti) only took about 2.5 hours, but it was hard and busy with trekkers. Towards the end of the walk my heart was pounding because of the thinner air. If you want solitude though, don't visit Annapurna Base Camp at this time of year. There was even a dog which looked to me like a Japanese Akita on the trail. We saw the dog coming down as we made our way up, and the next day it was coming up with another group as we made our way down. Some dogs attach themselves to trekkers for part of the trek, expecting to be fed by the trekker.

Many people were only walking to the base camp for the day, but our plan was to stay overnight, so we could see the dawn. The base camp was essentially four hostels, in the middle of the relatively flat plain at a height of 4130 metres, the "Sanctuary". As I previously mentioned the Modi Valley we had followed up for the last 2 days was narrow and deep, effectively a gorge in places. Because the valley exiting the plain was narrow, it wasn't easy to make it out in the mountains surrounding the base camp. Therefore the plain had the appearance of being completely surrounded by mountains.

Pic 11. Govinda, Mahesha, Genevieve, Tharpule, Tim and Ian at base camp.

Even in the mid-morning when we arrived the views of the mountains which surrounded ABC were stunning. There was also a steep glaciated valley of bare rock at one side of the Sanctuary, which fed the Modi River. Because of global warming, the glacier was slowly retreating up the mountain, leaving only a steep rocky cutting in the plain.

Here the three of us had to share a room again. However we were lucky to at least have a room. The tea house was completely full, and as I mentioned in Chapter Two, 41 people were squeezed into the communal dining room for the night, including guides, porters, tea house staff and 6 trekkers. No shower facilities though, but we had showered the day before, so in Nepalese trekking terms we were spotlessly clean.

Day 9, Saturday the 2nd November. We woke up at 6 a.m., climbed into our clothes and went out in the sub-zero temperatures to find all the trekkers, residents and guides outside. It had been snowing for much of the night.

Pics 12. Above and following. Some of the mountains surrounding the Sanctuary at dawn.

The views would have been spectacular even without the snow, but the snow made the view truly outstanding. As the sun rose it glinted on the hills, turning the peaks first yellow and then crimson. It appeared we were completely surrounded by snow-capped mountains, some with swirls of snow just above them.

It was a very hard walk down later in the morning. The snow made the steps slippery, and my boots weren't good for walking in the snow. Other walkers' sole patterns that I could see in the snow seemed more elaborate and to give much better grip - I decided to replace my 15 year old boots as soon as I got back. However, I did have walking poles which helped. We were often passed by groups of porters wearing only cheap trainers, so perhaps it was just me and not my boots. Govinda held onto my arm at various stages on the steep descent.

After we had descended about 500 metres the snow disappeared. It was a very hard walking day. In 8.5 hours we had been walking for 7 hours, arriving at Bamboo as it became night. Towards the end I was clearly exhausted and both Govinda and Tim offered to carry my day sack. Tim asked when I was feeling particularly exhausted, and ended up carrying my day sack for the last couple of miles to Bamboo.

We stayed in a fairly basic tea house in Bamboo. Nonetheless after that days walking I had no trouble sleeping that night. Amongst the other guests there were two French couples staying overnight on their way up the trail. They didn't have a booking and therefore had to stay in a shed in the grounds of the tea house. It was interesting overhearing them chatting amongst themselves in the communal dining room. The two girls were talking about their need for a daily shower and much better toilet facilities - we had a quiet laugh at them as we knew what was ahead.

One of the advantages of having an experienced guide such as Govinda was that he could always get us into accommodation.

Day 10, Sunday 3rd November. We walked from Bamboo to Jinhu Danda via Chhromrong. The stretch to Chhomrong was a real killer because of the steps. We walked down to the river valley, and then up innumerable steps to Chhomrong. We were now back in farming country. Not far from Chhomrong we saw some Nepal grey langur monkeys in the trees but we weren't quick enough to photograph them.

After lunch at Chhomrong it was down the hill to Jinhu Danda. Jinhu Danda was particularly attractive with lots of flowers around the tea houses, and is about 20 minutes' walk from a hot springs, which Tim and Genevieve walked to. I made my excuses, saying that as I had swum in hot springs in Iceland I didn't see any need to go. In fact I was very tired after the walk, and another 40 minutes' round trip sounded just too much. Tim reported that the springs had been too busy to be really enjoyable, but I have read good reports of them on the internet, so I would have gone if I had had the energy.

Day 11, Monday 4th November. We walked from Jihnu Danda to Tolka. This wasn't as demanding a walk as we had achieved on some days, but it did involve us going over some interesting bridges. It was the 4th day of the Tihar festival, also known as the "brother and sister" festival. We had missed the first few days, as we were in the Modi Valley with only trekkers and tea house staff for company. The Nepalese know how to enjoy themselves, a one day festival just wouldn't be enough!

The first day is the day of the crow; day 2 is the day of the dog. Although we missed day 2, various dogs we met on route still had marigold necklaces round their necks and coloured paste marks on their heads, called tilaka. Day 3 is the day of the cow, and day 4 the day of cow dung (strange to westerners, but obviously dung is very important to a farming community). Day 5 was the brothers and sisters day, where brothers and sisters reinforced their bonds. On several occasions groups of children operated little extortion rackets, singing and blocking the path on the excuse that it was a festival, and demanding money to let us past (in a friendly way). We paid 10 rupees on various occasions, only 7 pence or 10 cents.

As we got closer to Tolka a dirt road appeared, but with only pedestrian traffic. Govinda told us it had been built recently. Apparently it is left for several years to make sure it is stable and won't collapse in a landslide in the rainy season, before it is declared a safe road and motor traffic is allowed along it. It was a sign that things were going to change in the next few years along this part of the trek at least. Shortly afterwards we arrived at the Paradise Lodge in Tolka, an attractive tea house with good views of the trail.

Day 12 Tuesday 5th November. Compared to some of our previous days' walks, today was an easy walk along the recently created dirt road to Dhampus. We could now understand the logic of leaving the road for several years before allowing motor traffic on it – at one point it had largely collapsed several hundred feet into the valley.

We walked up a long flagstone staircase to the top of the pass, and then down a gentle slope through woods to the Paradise View hotel in Dhampus. A much better tea house than we had stayed in for the rest of the trek, and with an en-suite bathroom! But then again the Wi-Fi was not working, so no change there. Dhampus was however back to civilisation – we saw our first vehicles in 10 days, generally four wheel drive vehicles because of the quality of the roads. Dhampus was back to the land of the internal combustion engine, rather than walking and donkey transport.

This was the key day of the five day brother and sisters festival, and we were invited by the family running the hotel to see them performing the festival. This seemed to consist of the family sitting in two rows, one for male members and the other for female, facing each other, and painting a range of coloured tilaka marks on their forehead and exchanging flower necklaces and gifts of money.

After lunch, Tim and I walked about a mile along the dirt road to have a look at our surroundings. It was a fertile, well-farmed valley. During our walk we were accosted by four different groups of children extorting money on the excuse it was the brothers and sisters festival. The entrepreneurial spirit of the Nepalese children gives a lot of hope for the country's future in business at least! In addition to the Paradise View Hotel we were staying in, we passed hotels with names like Nice View and Excellent View. The owners were certainly showing a lack of creativity in naming their hotels. About the only view that was missing was "Bloody Marvellous View".

Day 13 Wednesday 6th November. We walked from Dhampus down to Phedi. This was an easy couple of hours' walk, albeit steeply downhill as we approached Phedi. We could have done this on the previous day if necessary. Phedi is a transitioning point like Nayapul where trekkers can join or exit the Annapurna Sanctuary trek. It has a host of small cafes and stalls selling tourist tat. Taxis were readily available, and we hired a small minibus to take us into Pokhara. The drive took about an hour and twenty minutes.

So we had done the trek in 13 days. We could, without difficulty, have completed it in 12 by combining the final 3 days walking into 2, but I would not have liked to try to cut out any more time. Whilst we could have done it under 12 days, it would not have been nearly as enjoyable.

Once back in Pokhara, it was time for our two porters, Tharpule and Mahesha, to leave us. They had been excellent, each carrying loads of up to 25 kilos up inclines where I was struggling to carry a day sack of less than a tenth of that. It is always difficult to work out what level of tip is appropriate. Since we had had excellent service we decided that $40 to $50 from each of us to each of them seemed appropriate. It is more than guide books recommend, but we felt they deserved it.

We decided to celebrate the successful completion of our trek. Lakeside is full of bars and restaurants, so it was time for a few beers and a meal. However, I had learned to avoid steak, having had the toughest steak I have ever eaten in Pokhara before the trek. I was told that as a Hindu country cows weren't slaughtered for meat, so steak usually came from cows that had died of old age! I don't believe it, but the one and only steak I ate in Nepal certainly tasted that way.

3. EXCURSIONS AND SIGHTSEEING

Pokhara

We did some sightseeing in Pokhara and Kathmandu before and after the trek. I haven't differentiated here between what we did before and after the trek, but simply sought to give a flavour of what we did and some key sights.

Pokhara and Kathmandu are very different. In recent decades Kathmandu has grown to be a city of more than a million people. Kathmandu is bustling – in fact too bustling for most people's tastes I think. There are wonderful old areas (see later), but much of the expanded city appears cheaply built, almost thrown up, with unmade roads, substantial air pollution and massive traffic jams.

Pokhara seems much less frenetic and a much more relaxing place to stay than Kathmandu. It is Nepal's second largest city, with a population of about a quarter of a million. The city is built beside Phewa Tal Lake, a natural lake extended by building a dam, in the Damside area of the city, to generate hydroelectricity. The main tourist area is beside the lake and called Lakeside (like Damside showing a lack of creativity in naming). Lakeside is where the low-priced tourist hotels, restaurants, tat shops and often counterfeit trekking gear shops are located. Trekkers on their way to the Annapurna treks stop off here, and Nepalese people just travel here to enjoy a holiday in Pokhara.

Dervla Murphy, one of the 20th century greatest travel writers, spent 7 months working in a Tibetan refugee camp just outside Pokhara in 1965 and describes it in her book "The Waiting Land". This book includes some photos of Pokhara in the 1960s. Pokhara was very different then. There was no road to Kathmandu, leaving the visitor with the choice of a 10 day walk or a short flight. The whole area was massively less developed, and the only westerners consisted of a handful of missionaries and aid workers, and a very occasional Dakota plane carrying tourists.

Not that Pokhara is just touristy though. Large parts of the city, such as the area by the bus station, are bustling, lively, dilapidated and scruffy, like many Indian subcontinent cities. At the same time, at various points in the city you can get beautiful views of the Annapurna range. It was also noticeably warmer than when we were on the Sanctuary trek, and in the early afternoon even in the first half of November oppressively so for someone used to British weather.

Phewa Tal Lake
There are a range of things to see and do in Pokhara. The lake itself is a major attraction. We had a very pleasant walk along the shore for a couple of miles, and returned via the town. We hired a boat, and were rowed out to a small island in the middle of the lake. This is almost completely taken up by the Tal Barachi temple, a modern but nonetheless attractive Hindu temple which is a major tourist attraction. We then headed across the lake to the forested side across from Pokhara, mooring about 50 metres off the shore to watch the monkeys playing in the trees with their young.

International Mountain Museum
You can take a short taxi ride to the International Mountain Museum on the outskirts of Pokhara (300 rupees to get in). This is a useful place to visit in the heat of the afternoon, as it is well air conditioned. It has good displays of mountaineering equipment through the ages, and of mountaineering in Nepal. There are also ethnic displays about the Nepalese people and the main tribal groups. One interesting display includes comparisons of peasant farming in Nepal today with farming in Europe 50 years ago, although I suspect some of the European examples were more than 50 years ago. Alternatively the display might not have been updated for several decades! One obvious attempt at Nepalese one-upmanship was a picture of a European farmer with a plough which is being pulled by two women, whilst the comparable Nepalese picture has the plough being pulled by a buffalo.

Pic 13. And which one is the Yeti?

The International Mountain Museum also contained a short display on the Yeti, including a ridiculous and naive "life-sized" model of a Yeti, whose fake fur seemed to be made from mop bristles. The display concluded that the Yeti was a phantom that did not exist. (If they do exist, hopefully they aren't like the model)! Don't let the Yeti model deter you from going though – in other respects it is a very interesting and professional museum.

Devi's Falls and Gupteshwor Mahadev
About a twenty minute walk down Lakeside, across Damside you reach Devi's Falls (20 rupees to get into the small park the falls are in). Then, on the opposite side of the road go through a gate to Gupteshwor Mahadev (100 rupees). Going down a winding staircase, you first come to a shrine to the Hindu god Shiva. Go further down and crouch through a tunnel to see the underground waterfall. It is sensible to bring a head torch, because some of the bulbs were out in the tunnel when we went down (and the Nepalese electricity supply is notoriously unreliable anyway).

Tibetan Refugee Camp
Another site worth seeing is the Tibetan Refugee camp on the outskirts of Pokhara. (Buddhist Shrines, display of carpet weaving and good for tat). The camp looks permanent, well built and comfortable. The Tibetans have been here for over 50 years, the main influxes being in 1950 when China invaded Tibet, and in 1959 to 61, when the Tibetans revolted against the Chinese and the Dalai Lama fled into exile. It is surprising that they maintain a separate identity after that amount of time, and considering that most of the population will have been born in Nepal.

There are also a number of one or two day walks in the foothills round Pokhara. However, having just completed the trek, we decided to concentrate on sightseeing rather than more walking.

Chitwan
8th November Friday. We took a TATA SUV to Chitwan. Chitwan is now a nature reserve, and was formerly a royal hunting reserve and therefore protected from farming and development. The SUV that turned up was not in fact what had been booked. Govinda had booked the same modern SUV that had taken us to the mountaineering museum, but a significantly older vehicle turned up, much to Govinda's annoyance. Govinda got into a heated discussion with the driver and then with the manager of the company who arrived.

However there wasn't anything to be done, the new vehicle was in use elsewhere so we left in the older one.

It was a five hour drive. Much of the way was on the road from Pokhara towards Kathmandu, and then we headed south from that road onto the road to Chitwan. We experienced everything I have read about in terms of driving in the developing world. In much of the west including the UK many people feel we may sometimes place too much emphasis on health and safety, but on roads in Nepal I can assure you they go to the opposite extreme and more. Large garishly decorated Tata trucks coming in the opposite direction were overtaking and therefore were on our side of the road. They seemed to be aiming at us, only getting back onto their side only a few metres from a head on collision. It was an experience I don't want to repeat anytime soon.

Pic 14. Some Nepalese methods of transport.

In Nepal a tarred road is referred to as hardtop, in the UK it would have been called tarmac. However the road we travelled on was in places potted and holed with the hardtop missing for hundreds of metres, so we were often driving on potted hard-core. We were told the hardtop had come off in the monsoon or because of the summer heat. Even when the hardtop was still there it was often potholed. Every so often we saw motorcyclists in the distance swerving across the road like drunks. When we got closer it was clear they were swerving to avoid major potholes in the road.

Tourists go to Chitwan to see a wide range of animals that live there. These include:

Asian Elephants. We rode on one, and saw many other tame elephants, and visited the elephants' breeding centre in the park. There are also some wild elephants in the park, and they are considered dangerous.

Pic 15. A One Horned Asian Rhinoceros in the wild. One reason for having a camera with a lens that lets you take a photo from a distance!

The One-Horned Indian Rhinoceros is the largest of the five rhinoceros species, and survives in northern India and southern Nepal. Chitwan has 500 of these relatively rare animals. We saw one.

Mugger crocodiles. A medium sized crocodile (only up to four metres!). We saw five.

There were three animals we didn't see, and in the first two cases at least I am very happy we didn't:

Sloth bears, so called because they were first mistaken for sloths. They are small black bears with a white marking on the chest. Their main diet is termites. They can be very dangerous, as they will often attack humans if they feel threatened in any way.

Royal Bengal tigers. There are estimated to be 150 in Chitwan. They hunt at night, and therefore are rarely seen.

Gharial crocodile. Gharials are truly bizarre looking, with long thin jaws and a bulbous snout at the end. Males can grow to 6 metres and 160 kilos. They are endangered, and there is a breeding centre in Chitwan which introduces young Gharials into the wild when they are considered old enough to have a reasonable chance of survival. We didn't visit the centre, but because they are such bizarre looking creatures I wish we had. I had to content myself with seeing a stuffed one in the Natural History Museum in London.

The Natural History Museum/BBC young Wildlife Photographer of the Year 2013 was won by an Indian boy Udayan Rao Pawar with a great picture of gharial hatchlings on their mother. See http://www.nhm.ac.uk/visit-us/wpy/gallery/2013/images/11-14-years/4727/mother-s-little-headful.html.

After our somewhat fraught drive we arrived at our accommodation in the "Wildlife Jungle Camp" hotel. Initially we were disappointed by the whole area. It seemed a bit of a building site. However, we felt more positive about the place in the evening after we attended a demonstration in the Community Centre by a group of Tharu performers. Tharus are the ethnic group of the area. Chitwan used to be a malaria area, and the Tharus have a highly developed resistance to malaria (presumably those who didn't have immunity died). The demonstration was actually quite good, consisting of local dancing and stick fighting, which the Tharus use as a martial art (the stick fighting not the dancing). Stick fighting was also developed as a form of defence against wild animals. There is a video of Tharu dancing and stick fighting on YouTube, in fact a similar demonstration to the one we went to. (http://www.youtube.com/watch?v=zGstOiBv2ic).

The next day we went on a two hour elephant ride through the elephant grass and jungle. We got onto the elephants by walking up steps onto a raised platform and climbing into a basket on the elephant. The basket could take four tourists, and there was also an elephant driver (mahout), who sat on the elephant's neck. It was cramped and rather uncomfortable, and a bit worrying when going through the forest. I could easily envisage my legs, which were hanging down from the basket, being trapped between the elephant and a tree. Nonetheless just going through the jungle and elephant grass and across streams on the back of an elephant was an interesting experience. We saw two deer in the trees, trying to blend into the undergrowth, but nothing more.

In the afternoon we had a trip in a dugout canoe. We saw five mugger crocodiles, three sunning themselves on the bank, and two others in the water with little more than their eyes showing above the waterline. Being one of nature's cowards, I found it a little disconcerting to be in a canoe less than 20 metres from crocodiles, but I have lived to tell the tale.

Later in the afternoon we left the canoes for a jungle walk, and were lucky enough to see a wild rhinoceros bathing in a small lake. The rhinoceros began to take an interest in us, and we quickly exited the area.

The following day we travelled by SUV (Govinda had managed to get us a better one this time) to Kathmandu. This journey also took about 5 hours, and with similar near-death experiences on the road.

Kathmandu
Like Pokhara, we visited Kathmandu at the beginning and end of our visit to Nepal, as Nepal's international airport is in the outskirts of Kathmandu. I am summarising the main sites we visited, and not differentiating between the times of our visit.
Kathmandu has a population of about a million. In many ways it is a sprawling and frenetic place, with cheaply built suburbs and unpaved roads. However, in the midst of all this there are also beautiful old areas with temples and historic buildings.

Traffic is a real nightmare. Like Australia, India, Japan and the UK Nepal drives on the left, but it isn't immediately apparent, Kathmandu traffic being frenetic and undisciplined. Weaving precariously between the cars are a large number of young men (it is almost invariably young men), on motor bikes. The noise was unremitting too – Nepalese drivers seem to lean on their horns when driving in traffic.

The main tourist area is Thamel, which is near the centre of the city. This is where the tourist hotels, restaurants, tour shops and shops selling often counterfeit "branded" trekking gear are located. It is noisy, dusty and full of life, but for the older tourist like the writer the enjoyment can wear off after a few days and you long for something quieter. Even Tim found it too hectic after a couple of days.

Guide books such as the Lonely Planet and the Rough Guide describe innumerable places to visit in Kathmandu. Govinda took us to the following five and a few others. In addition to Thamel, which has to be seen for its tourist bustle, in my opinion these five are the real gems. All charge entrance fees to westerners.

Durbar Squares in Kathmandu and Patan

Pic 16. Part of Durbar Square area, Patan

Durbar means palace, and the Durbar Square areas are the areas with the old royal palaces. They are more than just squares, they are areas of the city with the royal palace and temples. They are packed with traditional architecture and temples, many including extremely intricate wood carving. There are three Durbar Squares in Nepal, each in the capital of former kingdoms that are now part of Nepal. We visited two of them, Kathmandu's and Patan's Durbar Squares. Kathmandu's Durbar Square is about a 30 minute walk from Thamel and is a "must see", with its historic buildings and temples.

Patan is now effectively a suburb of Kathmandu. It is about 6 kilometres south of Thamel separated from Kathmandu by the Bagmati River, and is therefore a relatively short taxi ride. The Durbar area includes the Patan Museum in the former palace, which has a magnificent collection of religious art and artefacts. Patan itself is interesting. It hasn't had the same amount of new build as Kathmandu, and more of Patan seems authentically old Nepali than Kathmandu. There seem to be shrines in every street.

The Pashupatinath Hindu Temple Area
Pashupatinath is a major Hindu religious area centred round the Pashupatinath temple. It is on the banks of the Bagmati River, on the east side of Kathmandu near the airport, and only a short taxi ride form the city centre Entry to the Pashupatinath temple itself is restricted to Hindus, but a number of other temples are accessible. The whole area surrounding the temples is well worth seeing, and so is the general cultural character of the area. There are Sadhus (holy men who have foregone earthly possessions) who are happy to be photographed for rupees. Actually these guys do great business; they are far from being penniless! The area and old buildings seem infested with monkeys. Again, the intricate wood carving on some buildings is stunning.

The Bagmati River is sacred in Nepal in the way that the Ganges is in India, and funeral cremations take place on the banks of the river here. We saw a corpse on a stretcher with its feet in the sacred river (a ceremonial cleansing process apparently) before being burned on a nearby funeral pyre. It was strange to the western eye, but I assume no stranger than a western burial would be to the Nepalese. We

Pic 17. Tim joins the Sadhus

discretely took photos from some distance on the other side of the river. There was a sign asking photographers not to take photographs too close to the funerals, and therefore implying that photography from a distance was in order, but nonetheless I felt awkward doing this.

Buddhist Areas – Swayambhunath and Boudhanath
About 81% of Nepalese are Hindus, and 10% are Buddhist. These two religions co-exist in harmony in Nepal. If only it was so for other religions in other parts of the world.

Swayambhunath and Boudhanath are Buddhist religious areas centred round large stupas. A Buddhist stupa is a mound, often looking like a bell. Unlike a church or temple though it is not designed for a congregation to worship inside. Rather it is designed to hold religious relics. It is a centre of pilgrimage, and pilgrims walk around the outside of the stupa in a clockwise direction. Stupas can vary greatly in size; Swayambhunath and Boudhanath are very large.

Swayambhunath, or Monkey Temple as it is nicknamed for the benefit of tourists who find Swayambhunath difficult to pronounce, is a Buddhist temple area, with lots of Hindu input showing the interweaving of Buddhist and Hindu worship in Nepal. It is on a hilltop about 2 kilometres (a little over a mile) west of the centre of Kathmandu. The hill is covered in temples, religious buildings, and Buddhist prayer wheels, and offers a great view of Kathmandu. It is infested with monkeys (therefore the alternative name) and stray dogs, which don't seem to get on with each other. We saw packs of stray dogs chasing monkeys, who then mocked them from the safety of trees. Well worth a visit.

Boudhanath, or Boudha as it is also called, is one of Nepal's holiest Buddhist sites is on the northeast of Kathmandu, a little further out but within walking distance of Pashupatinath. It has one of the

Pic 18. Boudhanath Stupa

largest stupas in the world. It has been a major Tibetan Buddhist religious centre for about 1500 years as it is on a major trading route from India to Tibet. The religious area of temples and monasteries around the stupa expanded considerably following the influx of Tibetan refugees in the 1950s.

4. PRACTICAL ISSUES FOR THE TREKKER AND TOURIST

What Do You Need For Trekking In Nepal?
I can only speak from my own experience. A good tourist hotel in Pokhara or Kathmandu will allow you to store unnecessary luggage for collection on the way back. This is what I found I needed for a trek to the Annapurna Sanctuary in October/November: This is the basic gear and anything you aren't wearing should come to around 10 kilos. If you want to take your whole wardrobe you could of course just hire several porters!

A good waterproof jacket including a hood.

A down jacket for the cold. Alternatively significantly increase the number of layers you have. The temperature was down to -5 degrees centigrade on a couple of occasions overnight on our trek in late October and early November, but in the high 20s in the afternoon in direct sunlight.

A sleeping bag. At least 3 seasons, and preferably 4 seasons. Tea houses generally have blankets or duvets, but these can be dirty and/or damp. Take a sleeping bag.

Two pairs of walking trousers at least one of which is waterproof.

One set of **thermal underwear.**

Three base layers.

Several fleece top layers – more if you don't have a down jacket.

A **warm hat** for the cold, and a **sun hat** to protect your head from the sun in the afternoon.

Sun protection cream.

Two sets of walking socks and three sock liners. Sock liners are much easier to wash and dry than socks and give the feeling of being clean. One for wearing, one for drying and a spare.

One pair of good quality walking boots which you have worn in before the trek. This can be supported by a pair of **light walking shoes** to wear in the evening and as a back-up in case the heavy duty walking boots fall apart.

A pair of flip-flops for wearing in the shower.

A swimsuit if you want to swim in the hot springs.

Two pairs of gloves. One heavy duty and waterproof for when the weather gets rough and a second light pair for the slightly warmer days. The light pair should allow you to operate your camera without taking the gloves off.

A fold away, easy-drying lightweight **trekking towel.**

Toilet paper. You will only find this in toilets in the more expensive hotels.

Ear plugs. Even if you don't have to share a room with anyone you don't know, in some tea houses the dividing walls between rooms are one layer of thin and definitely not soundproof plasterboard at best.

A universal size wash hand basin plug. The plugs were missing from all wash hand basins whether on trek, in Pokhara or Kathmandu including in good hotels. A plug would have been very useful, particularly for clothes washing.

Antibacterial hand gel.

A metal water bottle. Sometimes you will buy boiling water, so plastic is not suitable.

Walking poles. I found a pair of walking poles helpful on occasions although I appreciate this can be a personal thing for walkers.

A head torch and spare batteries. It got dark about 5.30 in the evening, so this was very useful. Many tea houses don't have electricity in the bedrooms, and even where they do Nepalese electricity breaks down frequently. Not just in the hills, but in the main cities.

An e-book reader or books to read. An e-book reader allows you to take a range of books with no weight penalty and has a long-lasting battery.

A day sack for your use. The porters carried the bulk of the load. We had day sacks and carried what we might need during the day, particularly as the porters often walked separately from the group.

Snacks. If you are disciplined and can ration yourself, take a good supply of Snickers or Mars Bars. They get very expensive towards the top of the trail. If you are undisciplined and would eat anything you have within a few days, it is probably better not to provide temptation. You will just have to accept the extra cost!

Imodium or other product to treat diarrhoea, just in case.

Blister patches, just in case.

One of your party should have a **small first aid kit**.

Personal toiletries.

A small tube of detergent for hand washing clothes. They can often be hung outside your room to dry. Also bring some plastic bags to put wet clothes in when walking if it is raining, and hang them on the outside of you daysack to dry when walking if it is sunny.

Camera. Many readers will have a much greater knowledge of photography than I have but nonetheless I'll give my views. I took a compact systems camera. I wouldn't do this again, because even although it was smaller than a DSLR it was still heavy and awkward. I saw people carrying large and heavy DSLRs and lens, and I felt sorry for them.

I recommend taking a good quality compact zoom camera. This is much easier to carry and convenient to use, and has the zoom facility you would only get if you had a large and heavy zoom lens for the DSLR or compact systems camera. An up-market compact zoom's picture quality is indistinguishable by the amateur from a DSLR's under most circumstances, and it slips into a pocket, rather than hanging heavily from your neck. Expect to pay upwards of £250/$300. The zoom lens is also very useful for wildlife photography in the national parks, and "candids" of people.

If you need a new camera I recommend buying the camera in plenty of time before the trek to get to know its full facilities. It is just not effective to use it for the first time during the trek, as I did, when you are tired and rushed because you're trying to keep up with the rest of your party.

Make sure you have a sufficiently **large SD card or SD cards and a spare battery**. If you are like me, you will probably take around 50 photos and some short videos per day. In 20 days 1000 photos and say 40 videos. Check your camera's manual – some camera batteries last little more than 200 photos between charges.

It is probably best to take a **battery pack in** addition to the camera battery. The battery pack can be recharged from the mains in Pokhara or Kathmandu, and in some tea houses for a fee. It can then be used to recharge your camera, mobile phone etc. when on trek. Some people had small solar panels attached to their rucksacks, but my impression was they were not particularly effective. Try not to let your batteries and battery pack get really cold – they lose charge quickly when cold.

Insurance. If you are hurt or taken seriously ill on trek, being helicoptered out of the Sanctuary or Modi Valley will cost many thousands of dollars. It is therefore sensible to be covered by insurance, valid to the height you intend to walk to, and for helicopter evacuation.

Personal Hygiene on Trek
You will have to accept a significantly lower level of personal hygiene on trek than you would at home. In some of the more basic tea houses in which we stayed the only washing facility was a wash hand basin with a cold water supply situated in the open. Wet wipes can help though.
I also had my hair cut short before the trek as I didn't expect to be able to shower daily and I hate having greasy hair.

Clothes Washing Facilities on Trek
You can usually wash clothes in a wash hand basin using cold water, and sometimes hang them up to dry on the balcony of the tea house. However drying can be a problem – there are limited facilities, you are often on the move, and although it was sometimes very sunny in

the afternoon it could also rain or be very damp as you may be at cloud level at times. In order to help in the drying process I also hung my damp clothes on the back of my daysack so they could dry in the afternoon sun as we walked.

Water on Trek
When available we usually bought bottled water. However, this wasn't available towards the Sanctuary. You can however buy boiled water in tea houses if bottled in not available, and therefore a metal bottle is necessary as the water can still be very hot. I understand that some trekkers use it as a hot water bottle at night, and for drinking in the morning when it has cooled. We also took water purification tablets, and used them even on boiled water just to be sure.

Money Changing
Changing money is easy in Kathmandu and Pokhara, with money changing kiosks readily available in the tourist area of both cities. They accept US dollars, pounds sterling (although please bring English notes, rather than Scottish or Northern Irish), Euros and a range of other currencies. All kiosks we saw had a board outside clearly showing the exchange rates. However, it isn't possible to exchange currency on the trek.

Electricity and Wi-Fi
Power cuts are frequent, although some hotels and restaurants have standby generators, and the Wi-Fi is often down. It is better to be prepared for this eventuality, and carry a torch at night even in Kathmandu, and not be too dependent on Wi-Fi availability.

Bargaining in Nepal
When shopping in the cities, some observations on bargaining in Nepal might be useful. Westerners aren't used to bargaining in shops. In garages for cars perhaps, but not in shops. Also, there may be a reluctance to quibble over prices with someone who is significantly poorer than we are.
However, bargaining is the norm in tourist areas of Nepal, and probably if we can buy cheaper we will spend the same total amount, but on more things. The initial price goods are offered at in tourist shops is generally ludicrously high anyway.

I managed to bargain down a Buddha statue that Genevieve wanted to buy from 750 rupees to 250, and a handbag I wanted to buy as a present from 1500 rupees to 400. I reassured myself if the stallholder was making a loss he wouldn't sell it to me!

Taxis

Taxis are inexpensive and have meters. However I heard stories of tourists being cheated, and therefore like in many parts of the world it is best to agree the price before getting into the taxi.

Tipping

We had excellent service from our porters and guide, and so tipped generously compared to what the guide books recommend, with $40 to $50 each to each of the porters, and more to our guide.

5. WHAT EFFECT DID NEPAL HAVE ON ME?

I enjoyed my holiday in Nepal tremendously. Before I went I was a little worried by the physical and cultural challenge. However, they weren't as great as I supposed. The physical challenge can be dealt with by training beforehand, and the cultural differences in Nepal from the west just added interest and colour, rather than being a concern.

This was also the first major journey I had undertaken since I was diagnosed and operated on over several years for neuroendocrine cancer. Until the trek I had tended to play it save. The trek gave me back some of my old self-confidence. This was one victory for me over the cancer.

Had I not gone, those three weeks would just have been another routine three weeks in my life. Instead they are three weeks I will remember with pleasure for the rest of my life.

Also by Ian Douglas

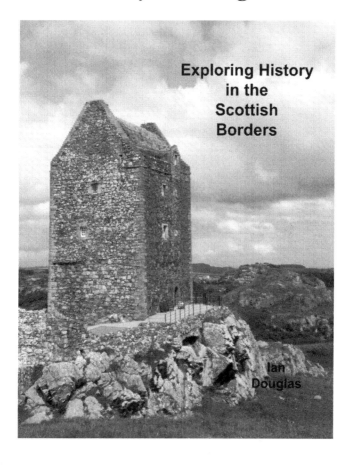

Available in paperback and e-book format. 29,000 words and 33 original color photographs.

The Scottish border area is steeped in history. This is the divide between the north and south of Britain, and the often fraught relationship between England and Scotland has left its mark. Centuries of war and bloodshed didn't produce Robin Hood characters, it produced a tough and often violent people, the border reivers. In the 16th century the Scottish borderland made the American Wild West of the 19th century look like a kindergarten.

Illustrated by many full color photographs, "Exploring History in the Scottish Borders" provides an overview of the history of this turbulent area. The Borders' past has left a legacy of splendid castles, beautiful ruined abbeys, and a depth of history few other areas can match. This book tells the story of the of the English/Scottish borderland from the time of the Romans, through the Scottish wars of independence, the turbulent 16th century and Henry VIII's "rough wooing", up until the reopening of part of the Waverley Line by Queen Elizabeth in 2015.

After centuries of conflict what was once the most violent part of the UK is now one of the most peaceful. It is a great place to visit - for many visitors it has more to offer than the nearby Lake District. Like the Lake District the Borders has beautiful countryside and strong literary connections, but the Borders also has a depth of history that the Lakes just cannot rival. It is also much less crowded and commercialized.

If your family comes from the Borders, you are looking for a present for a friend from a Borders family, or you are interested in Scottish history, this book should be of particular interest. Armstrong, Bell, Charlton, Douglas, Elliot, Gordon, Graham, Hepburn, Home, Irving, Jardine, Johnstone, Kerr, Little, Maxwell, Milburn, Moffat, Musgrave, Nixon, Pringle, Rutherford, Turnbull and Scott, and the various spellings of these names, are all key Border families. These families have shaped the modern world; their descendants include two U.S. Presidents, one British Prime Minister, the first man on the moon, and numerous major scientists.

Printed in Germany
by Amazon Distribution
GmbH, Leipzig